Welcome to the *Let's Learn English* Picture Dictionary!

Here's an exciting way for you to learn more than 1,500 words that will help you speak about many of your favourite subjects. With these words, you will be able to talk about your house, sports, outer space, the ocean, and many more subjects.

This dictionary is fun to use. On each page, you will see drawings with the words that describe them underneath. These drawings are usually part of a large, colourful scene. See if you can find all the words in the big scene! You will enjoy looking at the pictures more and more as you learn new words.

At the back of the book, you will find an Index, an alphabetical list of all the words in the dictionary. You can look up words in the Index and find out on which page each word is located.

This is a book you can look at over and over again, and each time you look, you will find something new. You'll be able to talk about people, places, and things you know, and you'll learn lots of new words as you go along!

Illustrations by Terrie Meider

7. Clothing; 15. People in our Community;
18. Sports; 28. Colors; 29. The Family Tree;
30. Shapes; 31. Numbers; 32. Map of the World.

Published by Passport Books, a division of NTC Publishing Group.
©1992 by NTC Publishing Group, 4255 West Touhy Avenue,
Lincolnwood (Chicago), Illinois U.S.A.
Manufactured in Hong Kong.

2 3 4 5 6 7 8 9 0 WKT 0 9 8 7 6 5 4 3 2 1

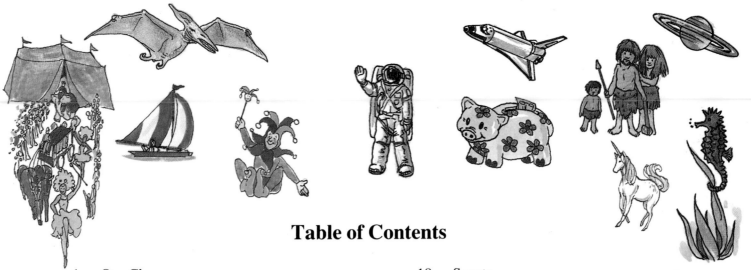

Table of Contents

1. Our Classroom

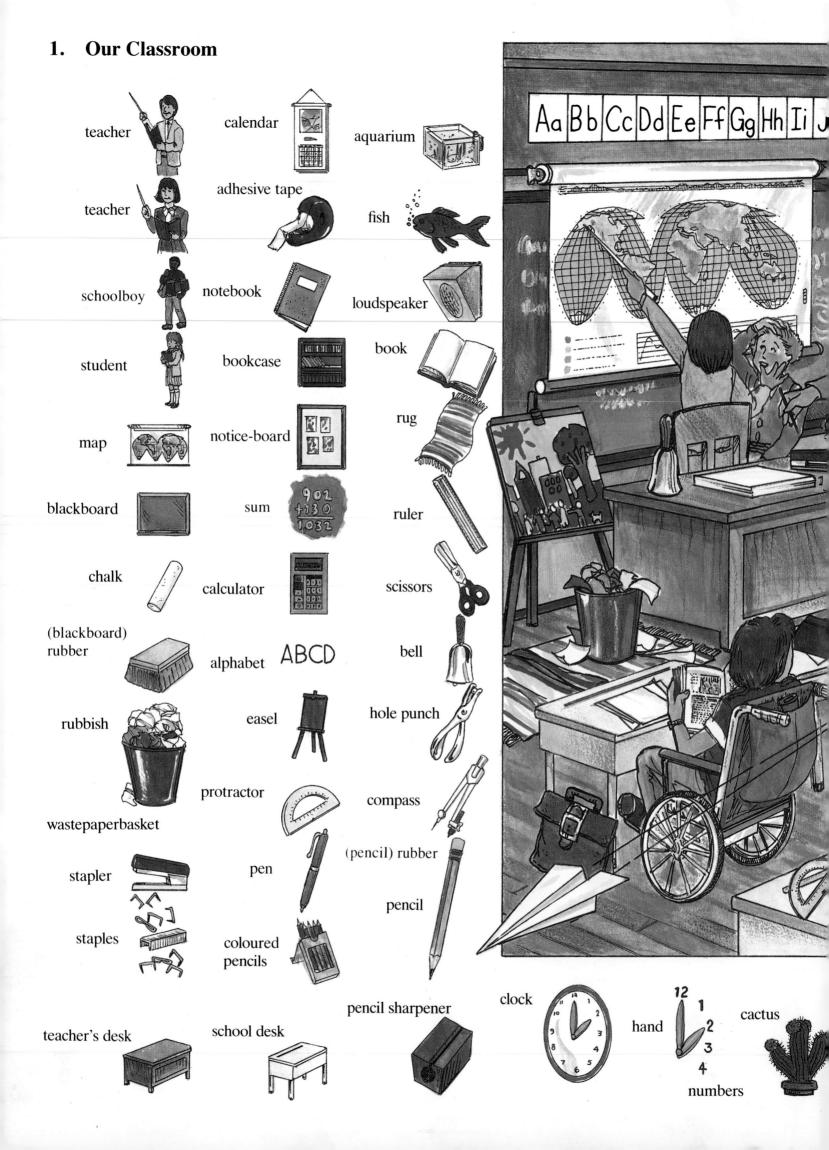

teacher

teacher

schoolboy

student

map

blackboard

chalk

(blackboard) rubber

rubbish

wastepaperbasket

stapler

staples

teacher's desk

calendar

adhesive tape

notebook

bookcase

notice-board

sum

calculator

alphabet — ABCD

easel

protractor

pen

coloured pencils

school desk

aquarium

fish

loudspeaker

book

rug

ruler

scissors

bell

hole punch

compass

(pencil) rubber

pencil

pencil sharpener

Aa Bb Cc Dd Ee Ff Gg Hh Ii J

clock

hand

cactus

numbers

plant   glue   globe   picture   paint   paintbrush   paper   crayon

2. Our House

floor

wall

ceiling

door

shelf

cupboard

hanger

window

stairs

medicine cabinet

bathtub

shower

towel

toilet

toilet paper

bed

blanket

sheet

pillow

mirror

vase

bedside table

alarm clock

rocking chair

curtains

venetian blinds

poster

chimney

roof

armchair

sofa

television

radio

fireplace

carpet

footstool

telephone

lamp

dressing table

record

record player

compact disc

videocassette recorder

cassette tape

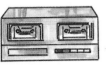
cassette recorder

bedroom

bathroom

living room

dining room

kitchen

3. The Kitchen

work top

oven

tap

pan

kitchen roll

chair

table

refrigerator

dishwasher

electric mixer

ice cubes

apron

microwave oven

freezer

food processor

drawer

spatula

flour

cooker

sink

kettle

toaster

dishes

sponge

washing machine

iron

screw

toolbox

washing powder

laundry

broom

mop

wrench

board

screwdriver

wood

dustpan

plug socket

vacuum cleaner

drill

sandpaper

flashlight

hammer

brick

ironing board

clothes dryer

nail

file

tape measure

saw

4. The Attic

trunk

game

colouring book

box

doll

music box

dust

jigsaw puzzle

ball of wool

string

skipping rope

knitting needles

cobweb

teddy bear

doll's house

ball gown

toys

comic books

top hat

whistle

light bulb

morning coat

cards

toy soldiers

hat

dice

film projector

feather

cowboy hat

blocks

umbrella

uniform

electric train

puppet

cowboy boots

magnet

fan

photograph album

cradle

marbles

rocking horse

chess

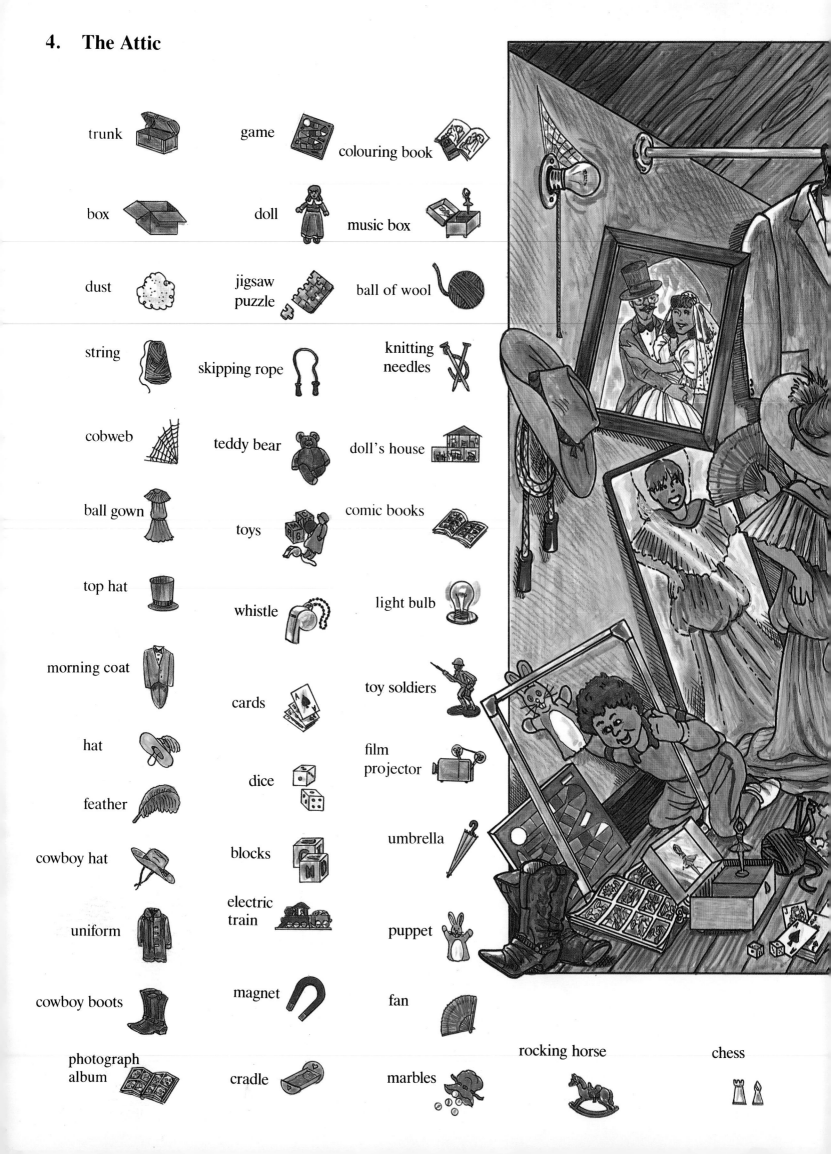

photograph

spinning wheel

picture frame

rocking chair

draughts

5. The Four Seasons (Weather)

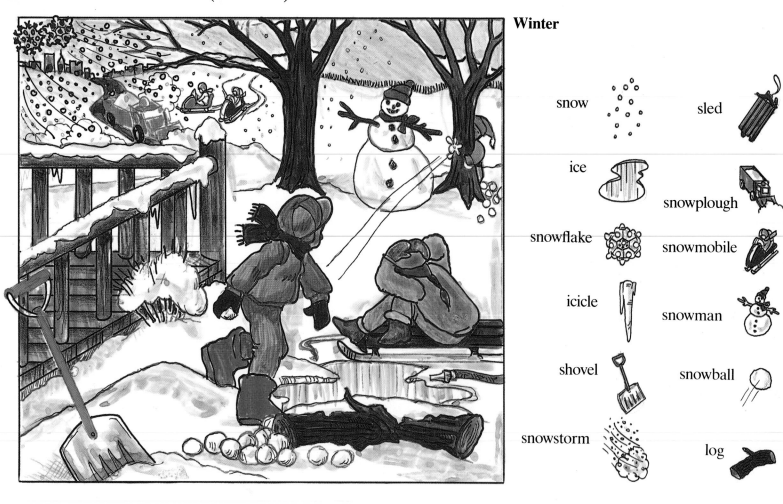

Winter

snow

sled

ice

snowplough

snowflake

snowmobile

icicle

snowman

shovel

snowball

snowstorm

log

Spring

rain

flowers

rainbow

flowerbed

stem

petal

bird

vegetable garden

worm

lightning

raindrop

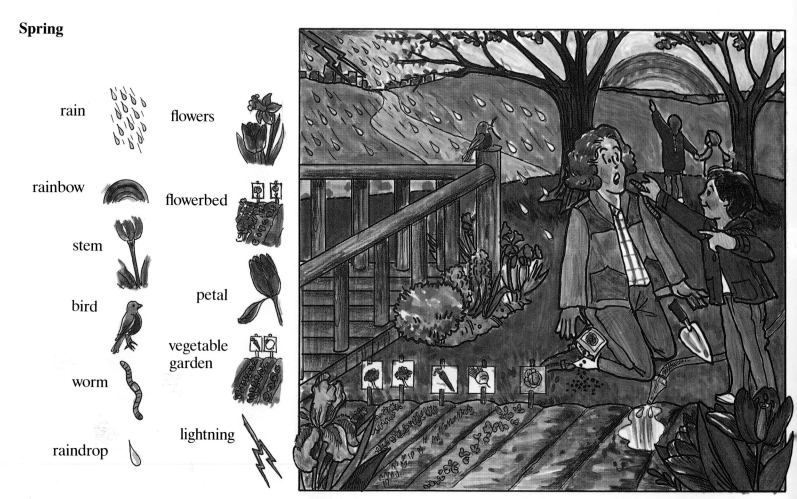

Summer

butterfly

fly

fly swat

fan

sprinkler

grasshopper

lawn mower

barbecue

hammock

garden

deck

garden hose

matches

Autumn

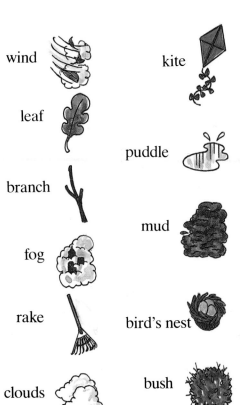

wind

leaf

branch

fog

rake

clouds

kite

puddle

mud

bird's nest

bush

6. At the Supermarket

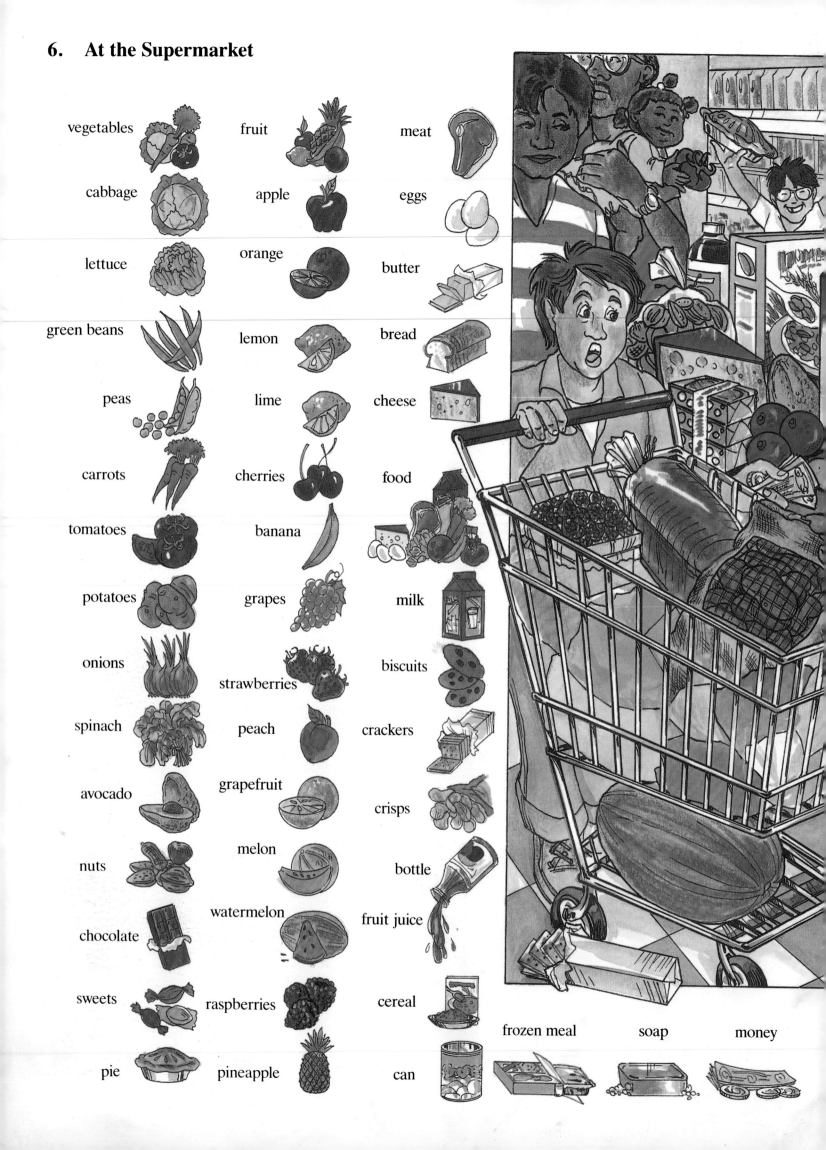

vegetables

cabbage

lettuce

green beans

peas

carrots

tomatoes

potatoes

onions

spinach

avocado

nuts

chocolate

sweets

pie

fruit

apple

orange

lemon

lime

cherries

banana

grapes

strawberries

peach

grapefruit

melon

watermelon

raspberries

pineapple

meat

eggs

butter

bread

cheese

food

milk

biscuits

crackers

crisps

bottle

fruit juice

cereal

can

frozen meal

soap

money

shopping trolley

sign

paper bag

scale

price

cash register

cashier

7. Clothing

glasses

buckle belt

trousers

collar

blouse

bracelet

ring

skirt

socks

shoes

underwear

tie

necklace

sleeve

dress

swimsuit

shirt

suit

button

earmuffs

gloves

handkerchief

coat

jumper

shoelace

trainers

tights

hat

sunglasses

earring

jogging suit

hood

raincoat

shorts

pocket

zip

sandals

rucksack

T-shirt

umbrella

boots

watch

body warmer

scarf

bathrobe

pyjamas

jeans

jacket

mittens

hiking boots

ski hat

8. In the City

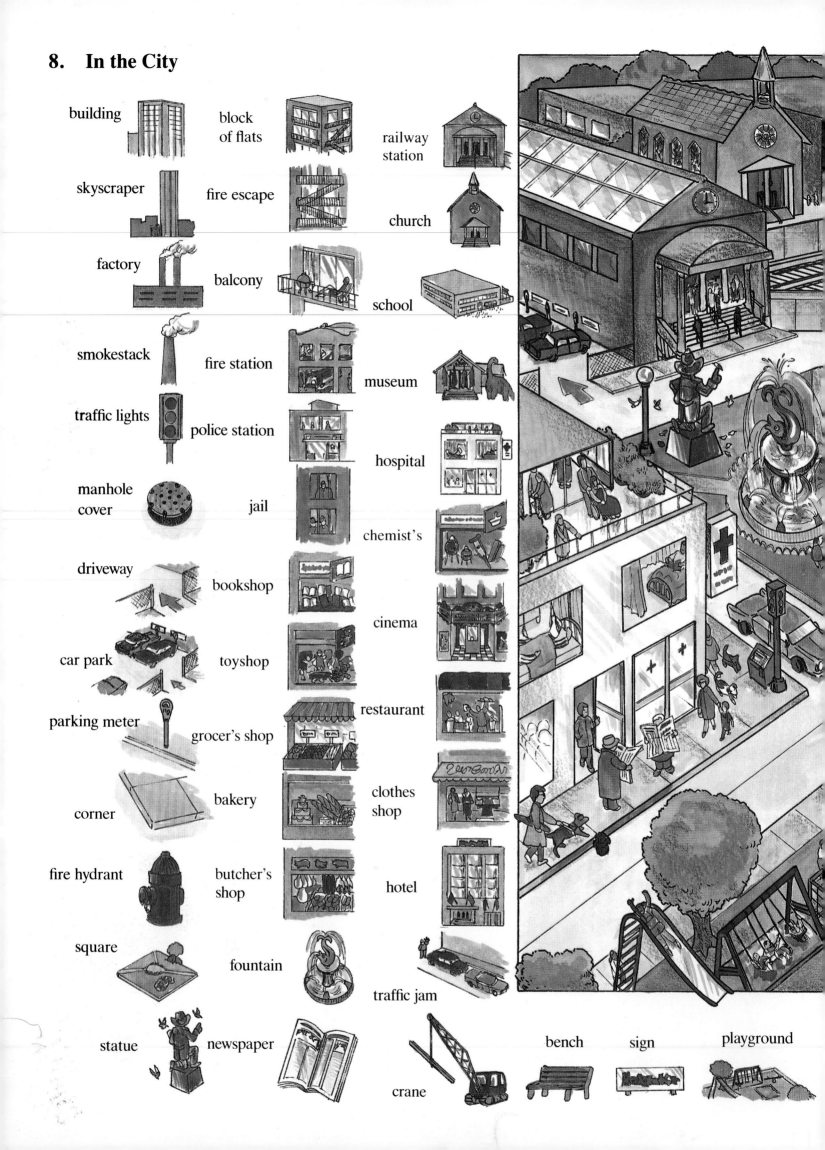

building

skyscraper

factory

smokestack

traffic lights

manhole cover

driveway

car park

parking meter

corner

fire hydrant

square

statue

block of flats

fire escape

balcony

fire station

police station

jail

bookshop

toyshop

grocer's shop

bakery

butcher's shop

fountain

newspaper

railway station

church

school

museum

hospital

chemist's

cinema

restaurant

clothes shop

hotel

traffic jam

crane

bench

sign

playground

park	climbing frame	swings	seesaw	slide	sandpit	beach

9. In the Country

farmer

tractor

barn

hay

dog

puppy

cat

kitten

cock

hen

chick

pig

piglet

rabbit

bull

cow

calf

horse

colt

duck

duckling

goat

kid

goose

gosling

sheep

lamb

mouse

horns

donkey

bees

frog

pond

grass

fence

tree

shadow

hill

road

smoke

picnic

ant

dirt

tent

sky

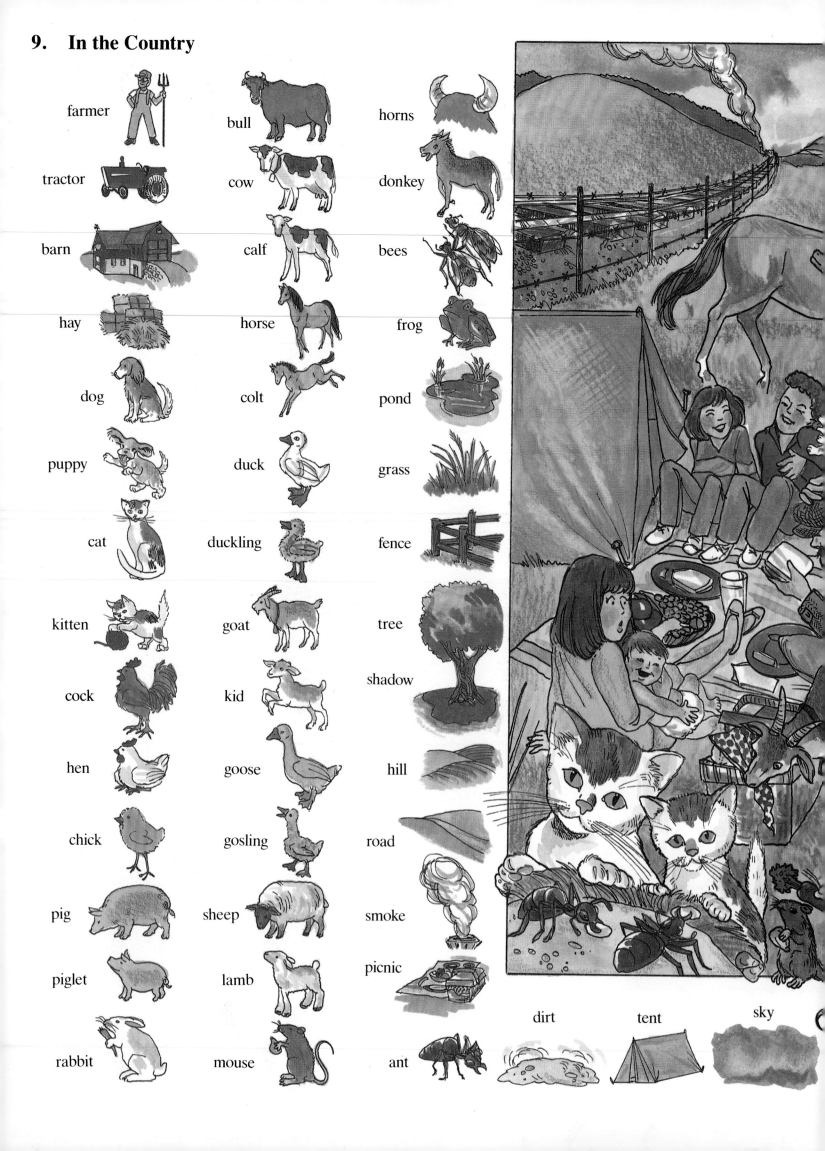

railway track

sleeping bag

man   woman   boy   girl   baby

farm

10. In a Restaurant

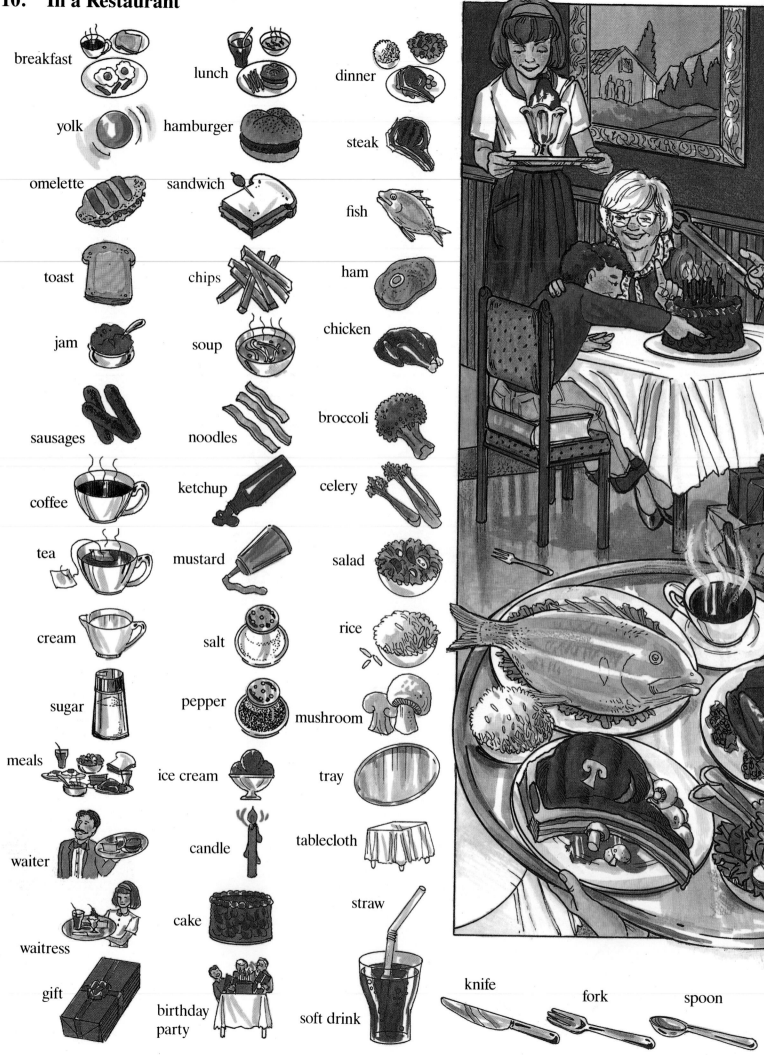

breakfast

lunch

dinner

yolk

hamburger

steak

omelette

sandwich

fish

toast

chips

ham

jam

soup

chicken

sausages

noodles

broccoli

coffee

ketchup

celery

tea

mustard

salad

cream

salt

rice

sugar

pepper

mushroom

meals

ice cream

tray

waiter

candle

tablecloth

waitress

cake

straw

gift

birthday party

soft drink

knife

fork

spoon

plate

saucer

cup

glass

bowl

napkin

menu

11. The Doctor's Surgery

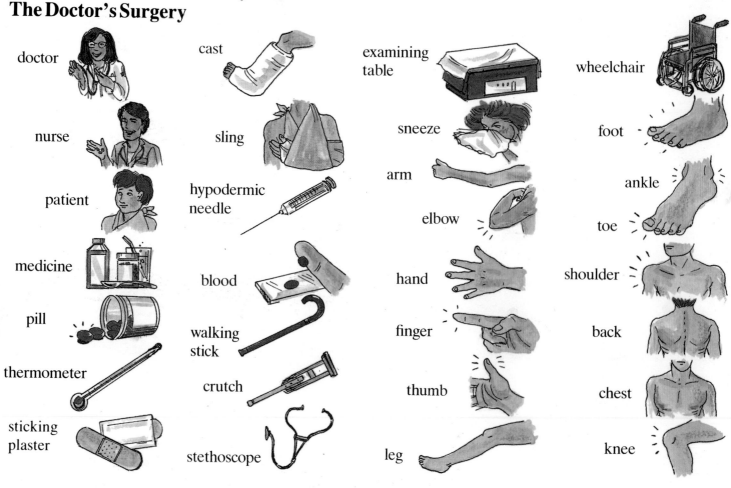

doctor

nurse

patient

medicine

pill

thermometer

sticking plaster

cast

sling

hypodermic needle

blood

walking stick

crutch

stethoscope

examining table

sneeze

arm

elbow

hand

finger

thumb

leg

wheelchair

foot

ankle

toe

shoulder

back

chest

knee

The Dentist's Surgery

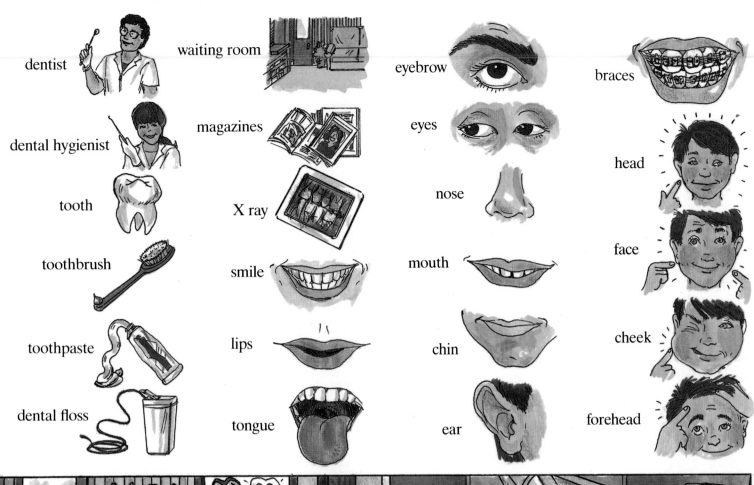

dentist

waiting room

eyebrow

braces

dental hygienist

magazines

eyes

head

tooth

X ray

nose

face

toothbrush

smile

mouth

cheek

toothpaste

lips

chin

forehead

dental floss

tongue

ear

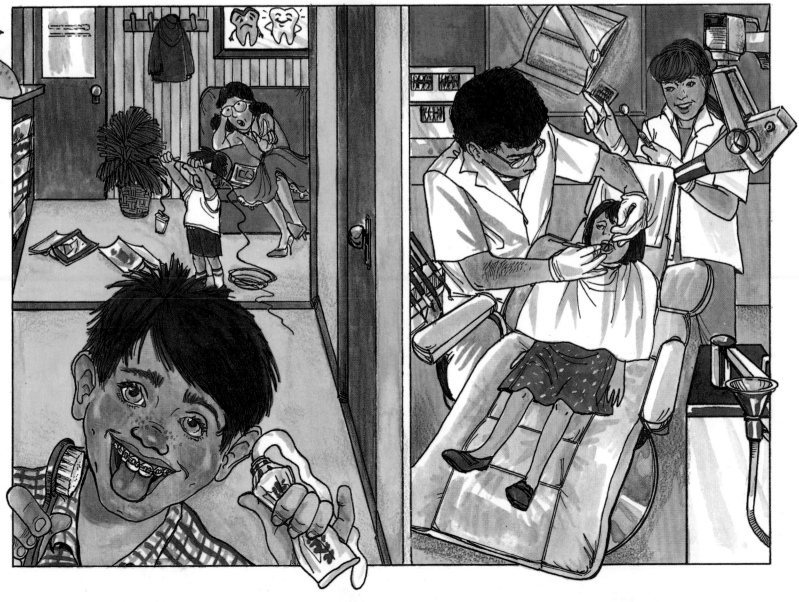

12. The Barber Shop/Beauty Salon

hairstylist

mousse

hair slide

shampoo

manicurist

plait

lather

fingernail

wavy

comb

nail polish

straight

brush

lipstick

curly

scissors

mascara

short

curlers

face powder

long

curling tongs

hair dryer

black

bald

brown

barber

moustache

shaving cream

blond

razor

freckles

red

beard

pedicurist

toenail

nail clippers

nail file

crew cut

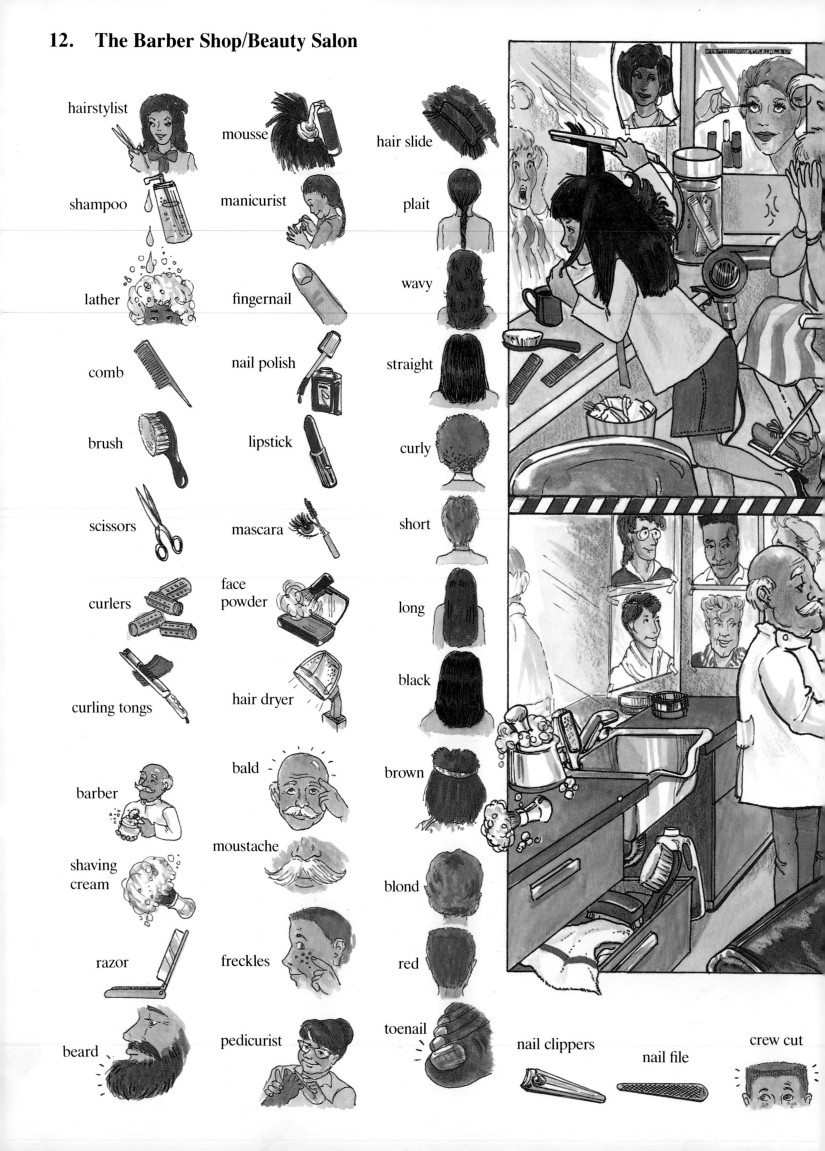

ponytail   fringe   bun

parting   hair spray   hair

hair dryer

13. The Post Office

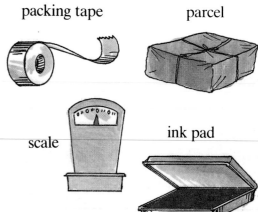

packing tape   parcel

scale   ink pad

post-office box   rubber stamp

label   rubber band

letter   postcard   string   knot   bow   postmark

telephone box   sender's address

address

9595

postcode

60016

postbox

postbox slot

postbag

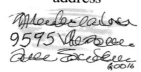 

postman

stamp

The Bank

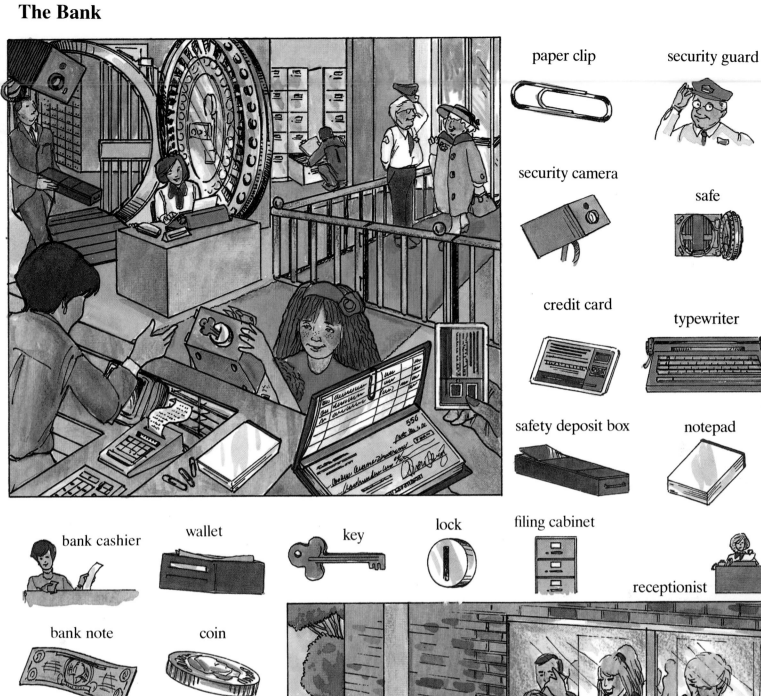

paper clip

security guard

security camera

safe

credit card

typewriter

safety deposit box

notepad

 bank cashier

wallet

key

lock

filing cabinet

receptionist

bank note

coin

cheque

cheque-book

piggy bank

signature

drive-in

cash dispenser

14. At the Service Station

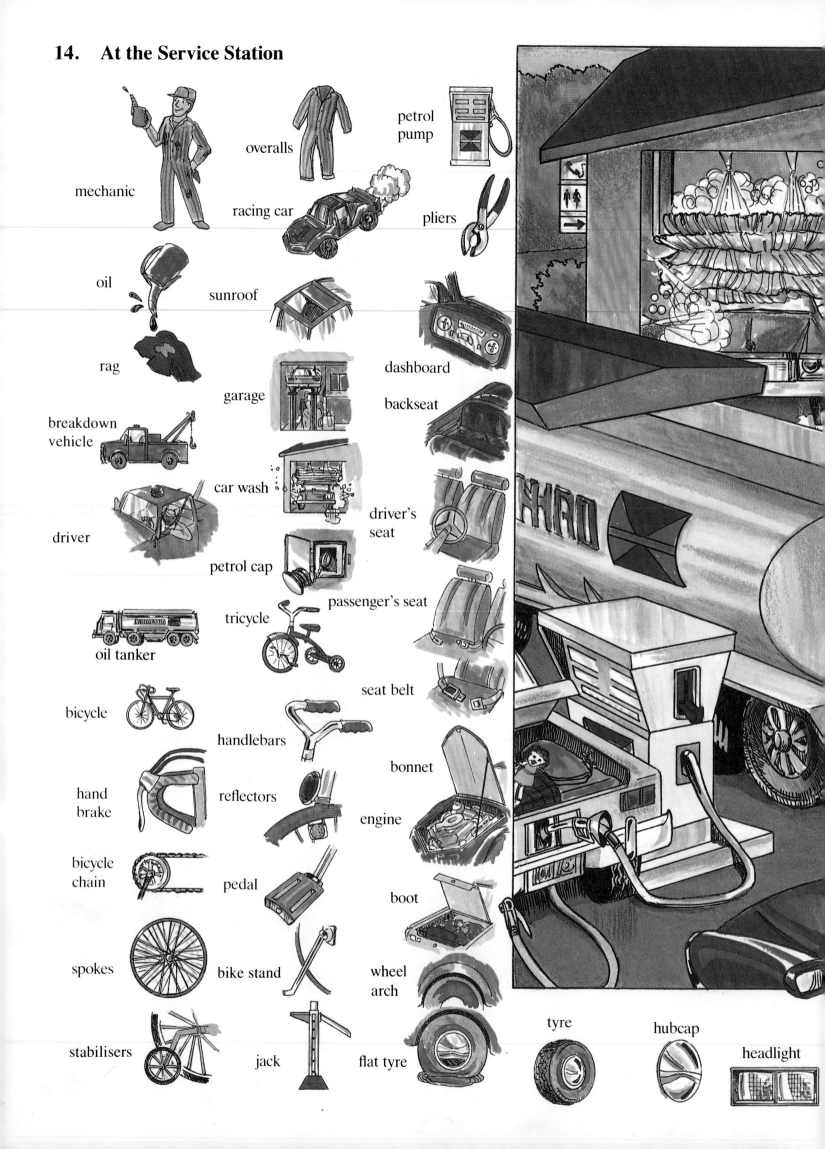

mechanic

overalls

petrol pump

racing car

pliers

oil

sunroof

rag

dashboard

garage

backseat

breakdown vehicle

car wash

driver's seat

driver

petrol cap

passenger's seat

tricycle

oil tanker

seat belt

bicycle

handlebars

bonnet

hand brake

reflectors

engine

bicycle chain

pedal

boot

spokes

bike stand

wheel arch

stabilisers

jack

flat tyre

tyre

hubcap

headlight

brake lights   windscreen   windscreen wipers   steering wheel   rear-view mirror   air hose   door handle

15. Professions

saleswoman

judge

cook

model

electrician

athlete

doorman

fire fighter

architect

bus driver

TV repairer

taxi driver

plumber

fashion designer

tour guide

bookseller

librarian

computer programmer

photographer

gardener

painter

salesman

secretary

weather forecaster

policewoman

vet

disc jockey

reporter

construction worker

florist

tailor

factory worker

optician

butcher

jeweller

foreman

carpenter

banker

artist

pharmacist

sailor

lawyer

paramedic

postman

cowboy

fisherman

astronomer

policeman

16. Going Places (Transport)

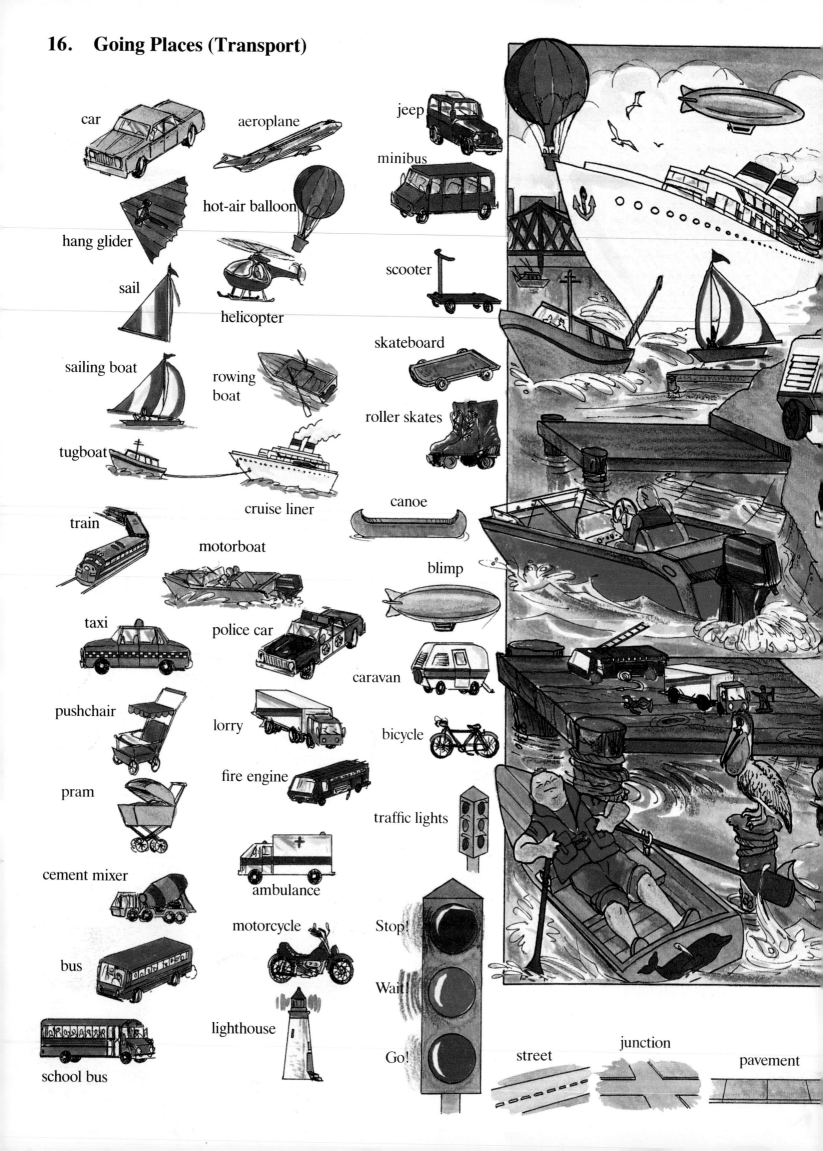

car

aeroplane

jeep

minibus

hot-air balloon

hang glider

scooter

sail

helicopter

skateboard

sailing boat

rowing boat

roller skates

tugboat

cruise liner

canoe

train

motorboat

blimp

taxi

police car

caravan

pushchair

lorry

bicycle

pram

fire engine

traffic lights

cement mixer

ambulance

motorcycle

Stop!

bus

Wait!

lighthouse

Go!

school bus

street

junction

pavement

 jetty

 bus stop

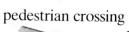 bridge

pedestrian crossing

 oar

boat

 stop sign

17. The Airport

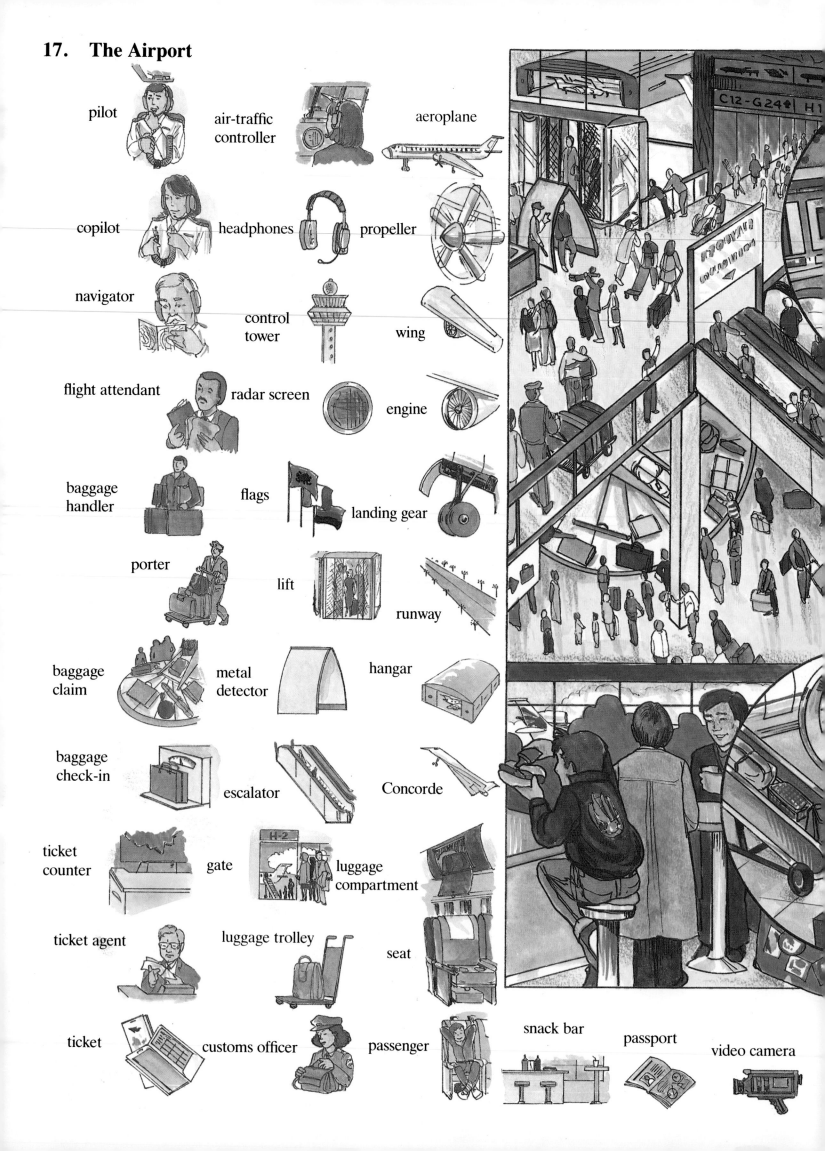

pilot

air-traffic controller

aeroplane

copilot

headphones

propeller

navigator

control tower

wing

flight attendant

radar screen

engine

baggage handler

flags

landing gear

porter

lift

runway

baggage claim

metal detector

hangar

baggage check-in

escalator

Concorde

ticket counter

gate

luggage compartment

ticket agent

luggage trolley

seat

ticket

customs officer

passenger

snack bar

passport

video camera

 tennis racket

 binoculars

 camera

 handbag

 suitcase

suit carrier

 briefcase

18. Sports

gymnastics

goggles

wrestling

cross-country skiing

cycling

football

long jump

car racing

baseball

boxing

badminton

net

skates

skating

hurdles

American football

golf

medal

horseback riding

baseball

jogging

ice hockey

tennis

diving

weight lifting

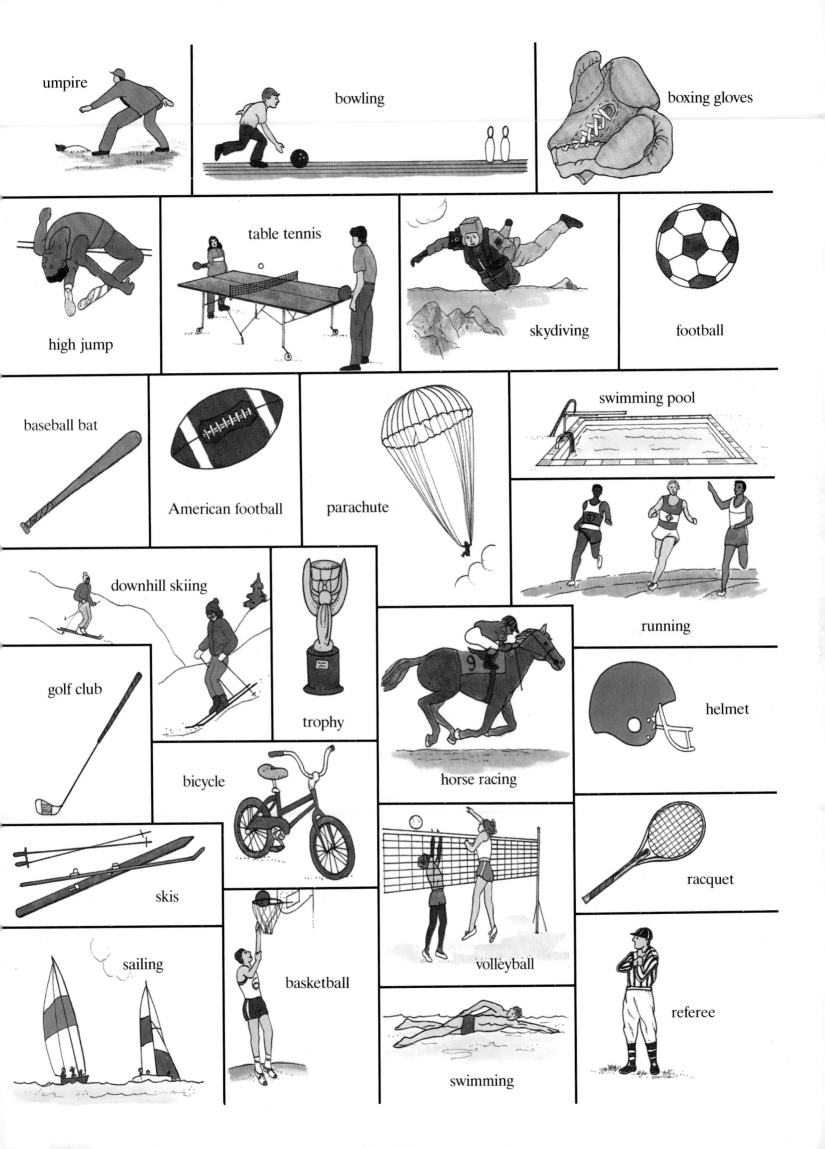

umpire

bowling

boxing gloves

high jump

table tennis

skydiving

football

baseball bat

American football

parachute

swimming pool

running

downhill skiing

trophy

horse racing

helmet

golf club

bicycle

volleyball

racquet

skis

sailing

basketball

swimming

referee

19. The Talent Show

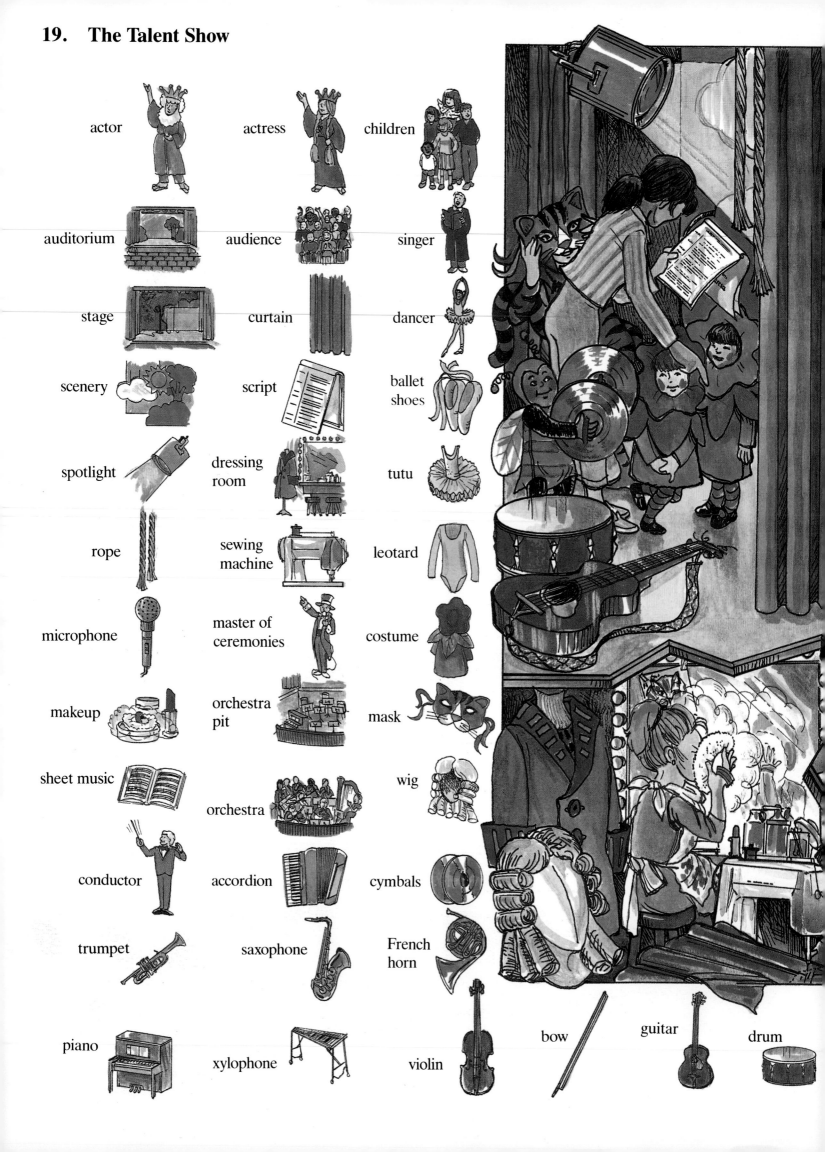

actor

actress

children

auditorium

audience

singer

stage

curtain

dancer

scenery

script

ballet shoes

spotlight

dressing room

tutu

rope

sewing machine

leotard

microphone

master of ceremonies

costume

makeup

orchestra pit

mask

sheet music

orchestra

wig

conductor

accordion

cymbals

trumpet

saxophone

French horn

piano

xylophone

violin

bow

guitar

drum

tuba   flute   trombone   clarinet   cello   strings   harp

20. At the Zoo

zoo keeper

elephant

animals

rhinoceros

ostrich

fox

lion

bear

wolf

tiger

bear cub

alligator

tiger cub

polar bear

zebra

jaguar

panda

giraffe

leopard

gorilla

monkey

flamingo

parrot

hippopotamus

owl

snake

kangaroo

swan

seal

deer

penguin

walrus

lizard

peacock

hump

turtle

eagle

camel

horns

wings

feathers

beak

paw   claws   mane   tail   hoof   stripes   spots

21. At the Circus

 clown

 popcorn

 toffee apple

 balloon

 peanuts

 film

magician

lion

tent pole

elephant

flashbulb

camera

juggler

tickets

baton

turban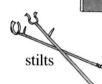

light bulb

night

ticket booth

stilts

big top

circus parade

toilets

bareback rider

tightrope walker

handstand

headstand

trapeze

somersault

trapeze artist

tightrope

acrobat

cartwheel

cage

ring

band

hoop

candy floss

safety net

whip

rope ladder

cape

lion tamer

unicycle

rope

ringmaster

22. In the Ocean

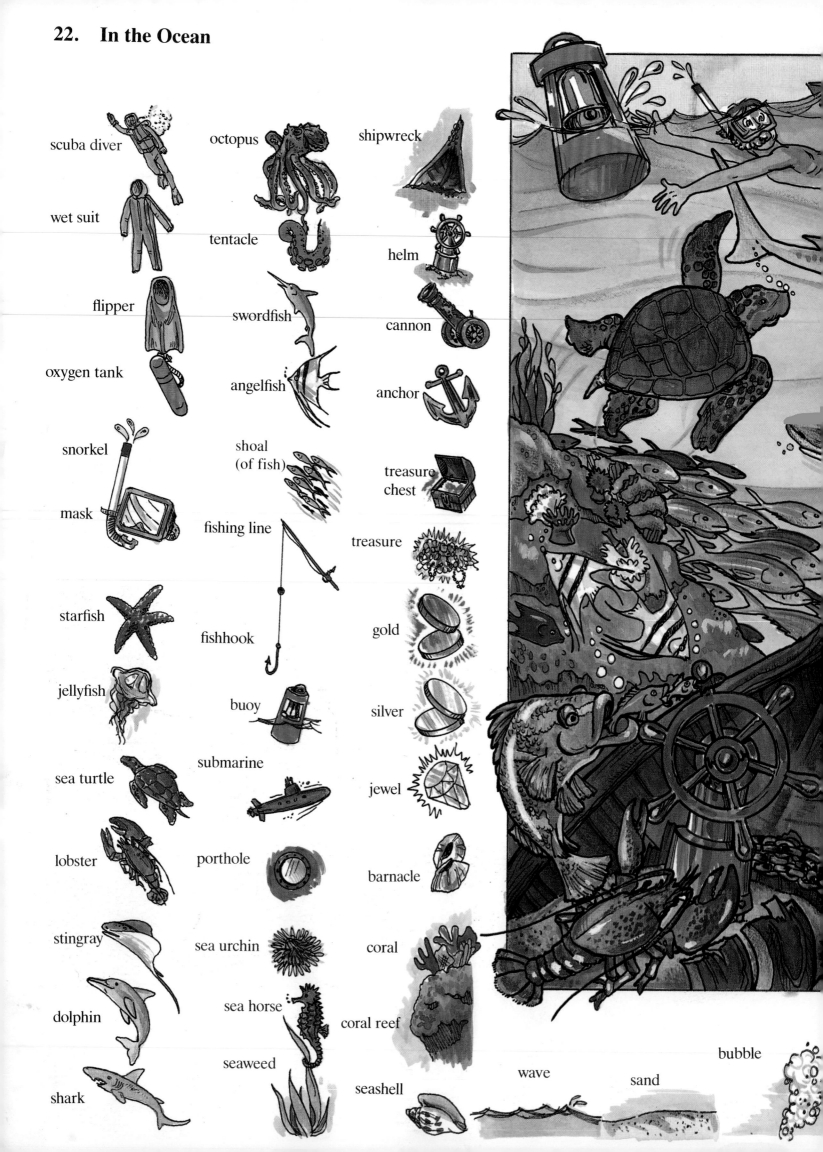

scuba diver

wet suit

flipper

oxygen tank

snorkel

mask

starfish

jellyfish

sea turtle

lobster

stingray

dolphin

shark

octopus

tentacle

swordfish

angelfish

shoal
(of fish)

fishing line

fishhook

buoy

submarine

porthole

sea urchin

sea horse

seaweed

shipwreck

helm

cannon

anchor

treasure
chest

treasure

gold

silver

jewel

barnacle

coral

coral reef

seashell

wave

sand

bubble

scales

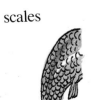

gills

fin

clam

crab

squid

whale

23. Space

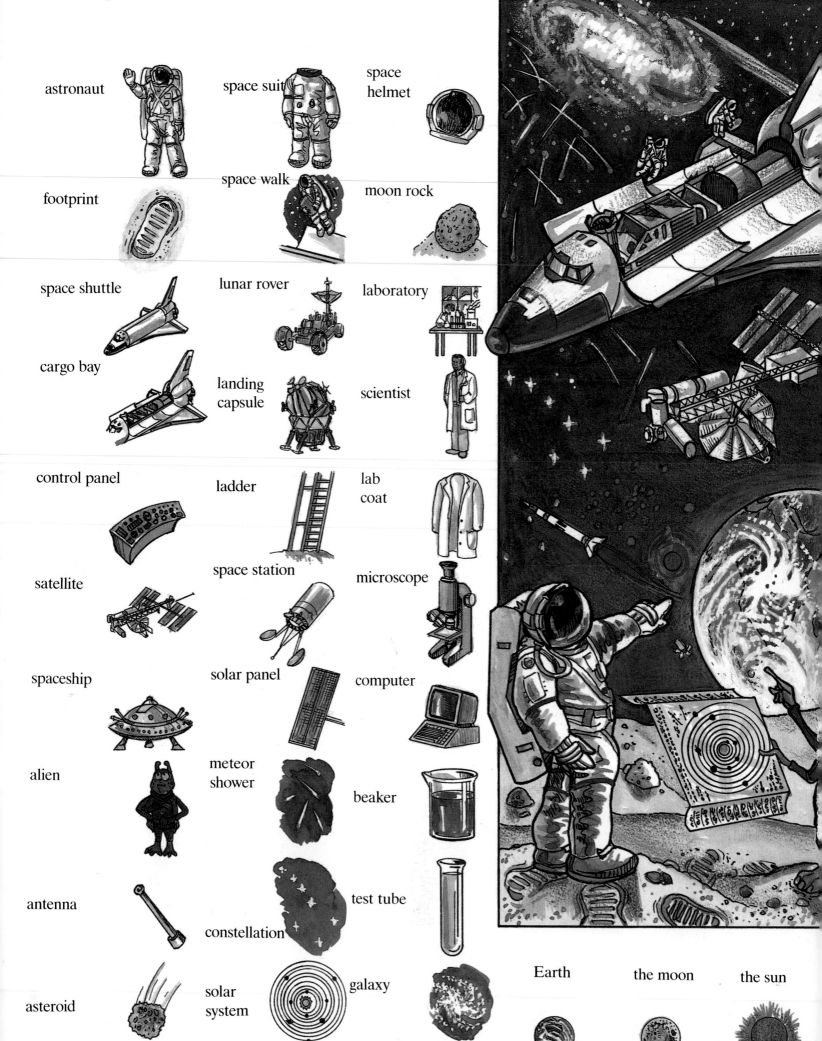

astronaut

space suit

space helmet

footprint

space walk

moon rock

space shuttle

lunar rover

laboratory

cargo bay

landing capsule

scientist

control panel

ladder

lab coat

satellite

space station

microscope

spaceship

solar panel

computer

alien

meteor shower

beaker

antenna

test tube

constellation

asteroid

solar system

galaxy

Earth

the moon

the sun

planet   rings

crater   stars   comet   nebula   rocket

robot

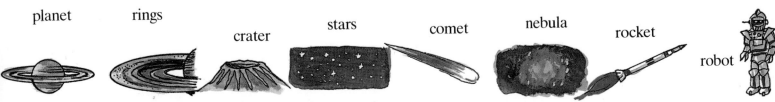

24. Human History

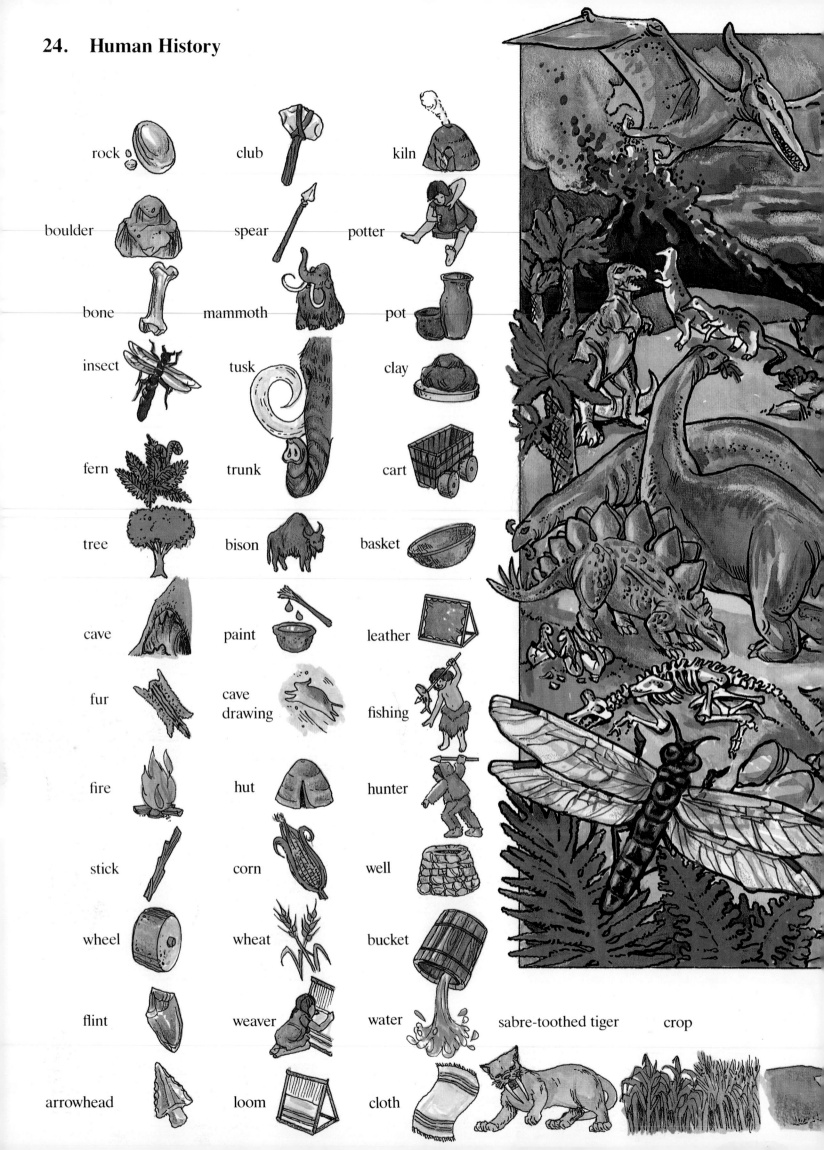

rock

boulder

bone

insect

fern

tree

cave

fur

fire

stick

wheel

flint

arrowhead

club

spear

mammoth

tusk

trunk

bison

paint

cave
drawing

hut

corn

wheat

weaver

loom

kiln

potter

pot

clay

cart

basket

leather

fishing

hunter

well

bucket

water

cloth

sabre-toothed tiger

crop

field   village   cave dwellers   skeleton   dinosaur   pterodactyl

25.   The Make-Believe Castle

banner

squire

court jester

dragon

knight

minstrel

magic wand

armour

unicorn

fairy

chain mail

lance

elf

forest

shield

giant

saddle

axe

forge

stirrup

sword

blacksmith

reins

bow

anvil

stable

arrow

horseshoe

dungeon

quiver

tower

moat

archer

courtyard

castle

bat

rat

crown

drawbridge

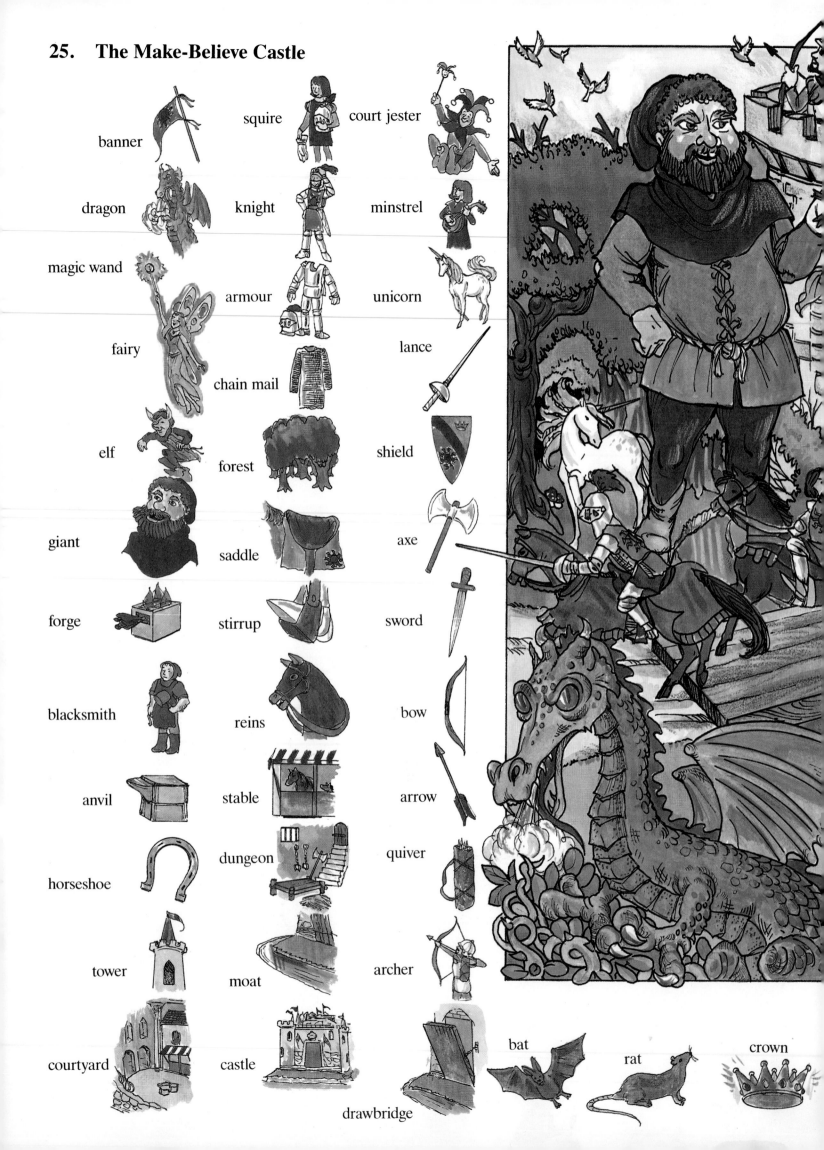

king   queen   princess   prince   throne   spider   spider's web

26. The Mouse Hunt (Prepositions and Adjectives)

behind

good

above

on top of

in front of

inside

outside

bad

under

next to

soft

tall

wide

narrow

heavy

short

difficult

large

medium

small

dry

wet

fat

full

empty

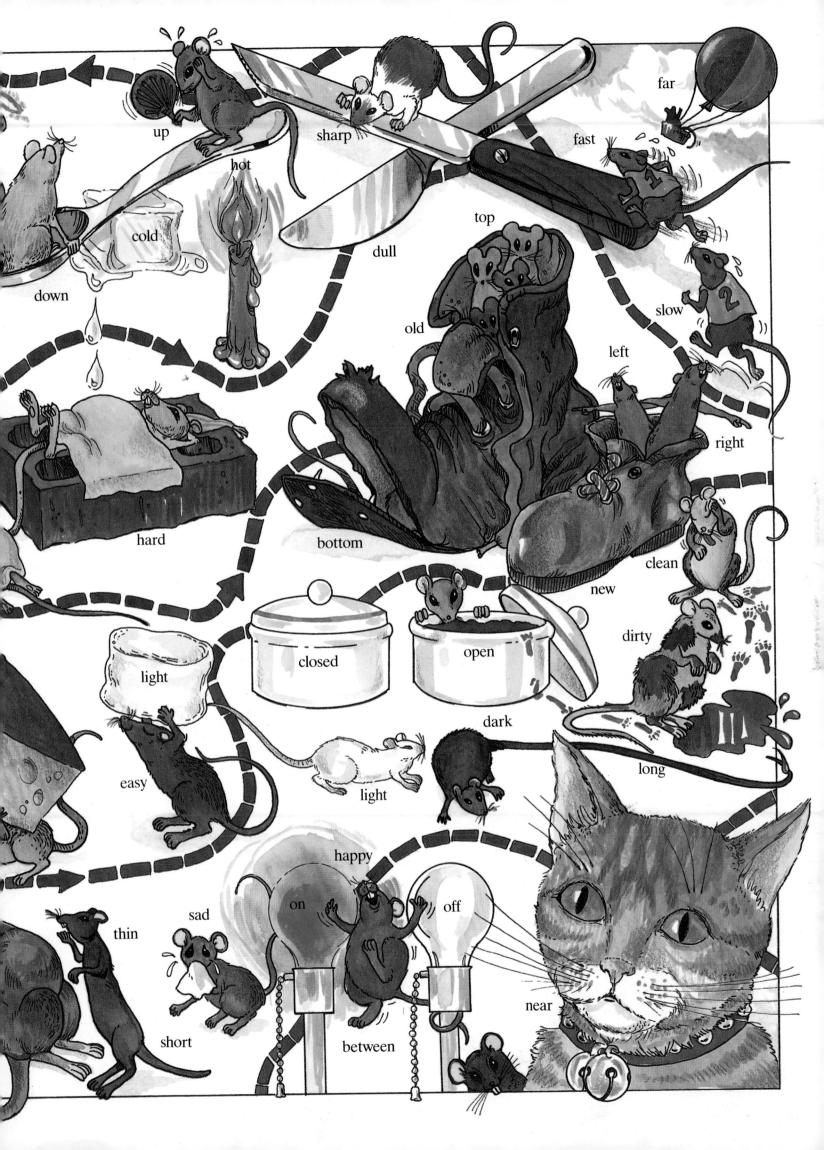

27.   Action Words

to drink   to eat   to sleep   to wash   to skate

to fall   to cry   to laugh   to fly   to write

to read   to play (a game)   to play (an instrument)   to sit down   to stand up

to dance   to walk   to run   to climb   to jump

to drive   to push   to sell   to buy   to ski

to dive   to swim   to paint   to draw   to ride a bicycle

to come   to go   to throw   to catch   to watch

to sing   to talk   to kick   to listen (to)   to think

to roar   to dig   to pour   to juggle   to point (at)

to look for   to find   to give   to receive   to cut

to cook   to open   to close   to take a bath   to teach

to break   to mend   to carry   to pull   to wait

28. Colours

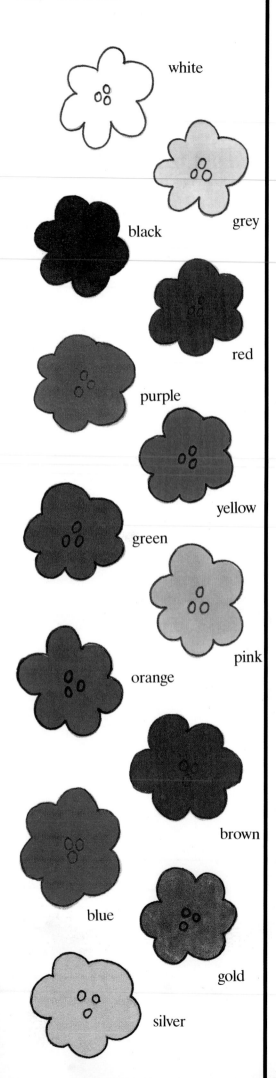

white

grey

black

red

purple

yellow

green

pink

orange

brown

blue

gold

silver

29. The Family Tree

grandmother, granny

father, dad

mother, mum

son

brother

sister

grandfather, grandad

uncle

aunt

cousin

cousin

daughter

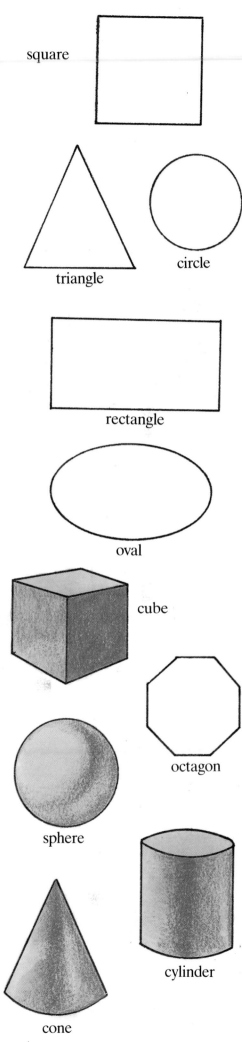

square

triangle

circle

rectangle

oval

cube

octagon

sphere

cylinder

cone

31. Numbers

Ordinal Numbers

tenth

ninth

eighth

sixth

seventh

fifth

fourth

second

third

first

Cardinal Numbers

0 zero	½ one-half	1 one	2 two	3 three	4 four	5 five	6 six

16 sixteen	17 seventeen	18 eighteen	19 nineteen	20 twenty	21 twenty-one

28 twenty-eight	29 twenty-nine	30 thirty	31 thirty-one
37 thirty-seven	38 thirty-eight	39 thirty-nine	40 forty
46 forty-six	47 forty-seven	48 forty-eight	49 forty-nine
55 fifty-five	56 fifty-six	57 fifty-seven	58 fifty-eight
64 sixty-four	65 sixty-five	66 sixty-six	67 sixty-seven
73 seventy-three	74 seventy-four	75 seventy-five	76 seventy-six
82 eighty-two	83 eighty-three	84 eighty-four	85 eighty-five
91 ninety-one	92 ninety-two	93 ninety-three	94 ninety-four

100 one hundred	1,000 one thousand	10,000 ten thousand

| **7** seven | **8** eight | **9** nine | **10** ten | **11** eleven | **12** twelve | **13** thirteen | **14** fourteen | **15** fifteen |

| **22** twenty-two | **23** twenty-three | **24** twenty-four | **25** twenty-five | **26** twenty-six | **27** twenty-seven |

| **32** thirty-two | **33** thirty-three | **34** thirty-four | **35** thirty-five | **36** thirty-six |

| **41** forty-one | **42** forty-two | **43** forty-three | **44** forty-four | **45** forty-five |

| **50** fifty | **51** fifty-one | **52** fifty-two | **53** fifty-three | **54** fifty-four |

| **59** fifty-nine | **60** sixty | **61** sixty-one | **62** sixty-two | **63** sixty-three |

| **68** sixty-eight | **69** sixty-nine | **70** seventy | **71** seventy-one | **72** seventy-two |

| **77** seventy-seven | **78** seventy-eight | **79** seventy-nine | **80** eighty | **81** eighty-one |

| **86** eighty-six | **87** eighty-seven | **88** eighty-eight | **89** eighty-nine | **90** ninety |

| **95** ninety-five | **96** ninety-six | **97** ninety-seven | **98** ninety-eight | **99** ninety-nine |

100,000 one hundred thousand   **1,000,000** one million   **1,000,000,000** one billion

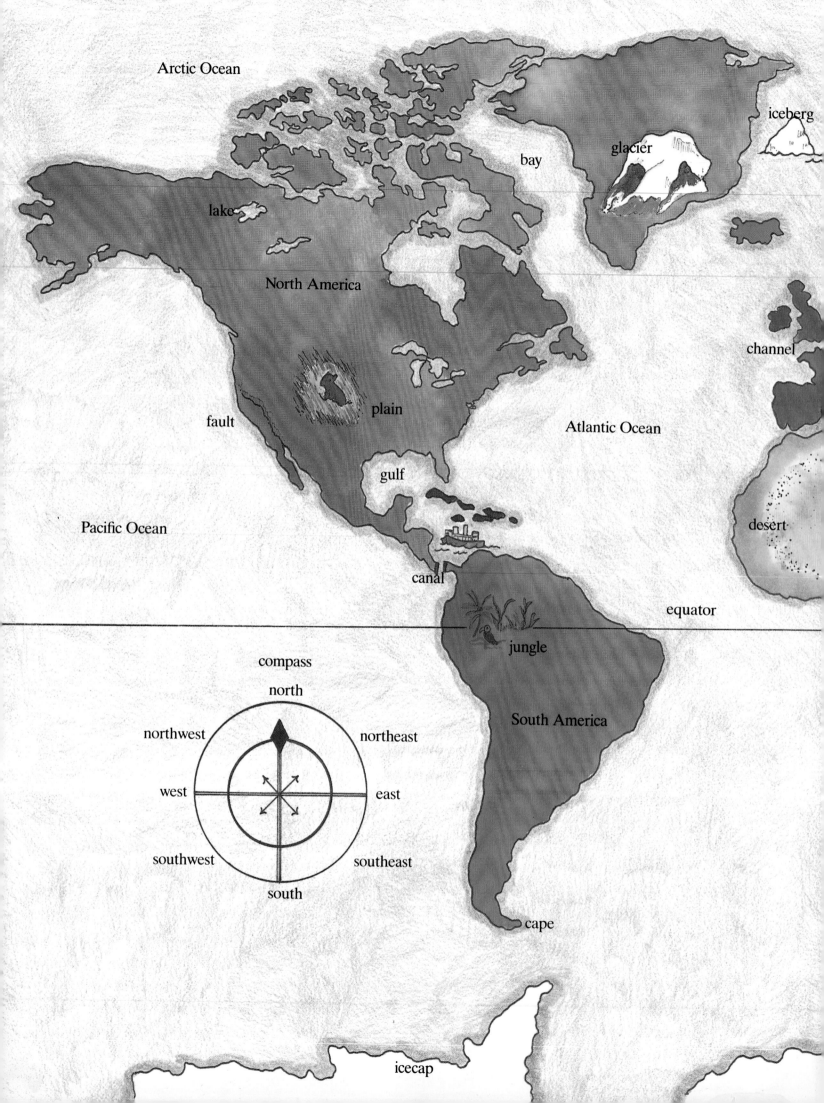

Arctic Ocean

iceberg

glacier

bay

lake

North America

channel

plain

fault

Atlantic Ocean

gulf

desert

Pacific Ocean

canal

equator

jungle

compass

north

South America

northwest

northeast

west

east

southwest

southeast

cape

south

icecap

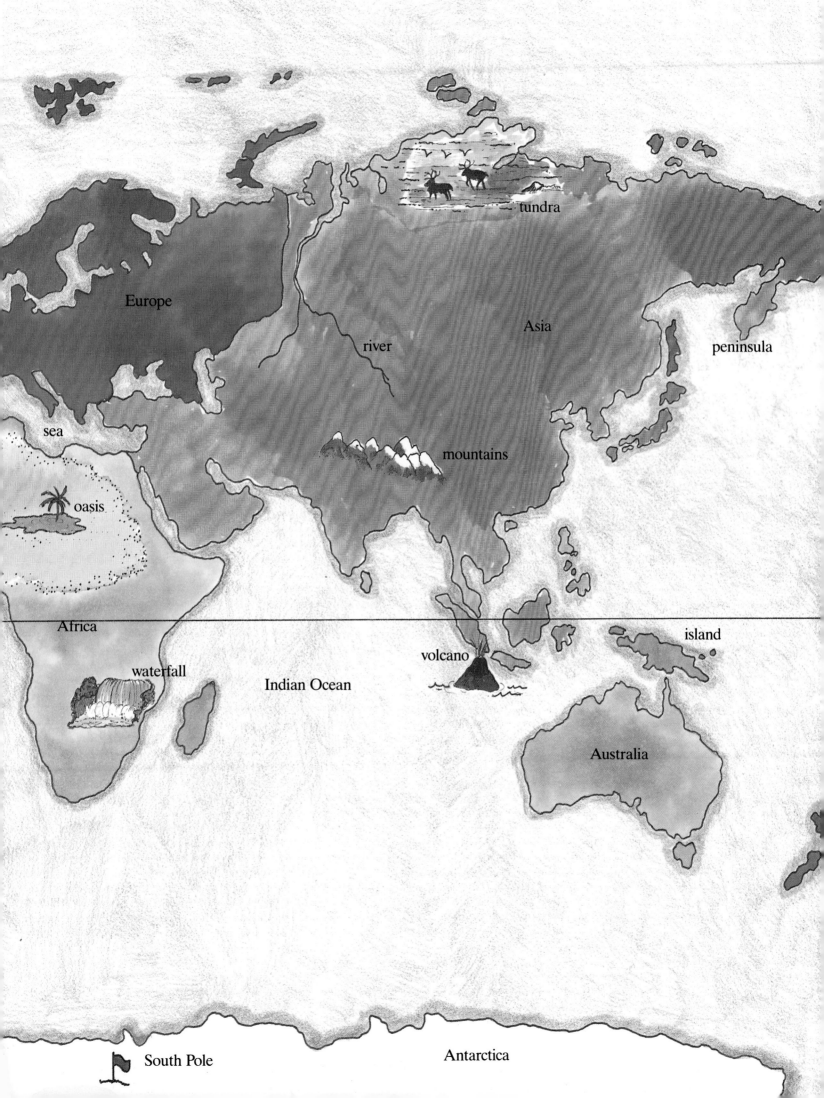

North Pole

tundra

Europe

Asia

river

peninsula

sea

mountains

oasis

Africa

island

volcano

waterfall

Indian Ocean

Australia

South Pole

Antarctica

Index

This index is a list of all words in the dictionary in alphabetical order. After each word, you will find the number of the picture in which you can find the word.